# When Apples aren't Enough

# When Apples aren't Enough

Tania Mouscardy-Johnson

©2014, Tania Mouscardy-Johnson. Except as provided by the Copyright Act [2014, Tania Mouscardy-Johnson] no part of this publication may be reproduced, stored in a retrieval system or transmitted in any form or by any means without the prior written permission of the publisher.

ISBN: 098614939X
ISBN 13: 9780986149399

*With love,*
*For my family, John, Christopher, Nicholas and Katelynn Carroll-Johnson*
*For my parents, Mr. and Mrs. Jean and Gisele Mouscardy & Mrs. Barbara Johnson*
*For my Catch-up Buddy, Richard Wagner*

*Deepest Gratitude and Love to: Dr. Elaine Margarita (My Heroine), Dr. Kevin Simmons (My Champion), and Carole Oligario (my perpetual cheerleader/critic)*

*Acknowledgement and Love to: Christian Harrigan, Heather Geoghan, Laura Canino, Lorene Bossong, Luca Lucano, Denise Silver, Pat Longo (the Dove), Lyn Cavataio, James Kassebaum, Kevin Bonanno, Patricia Wingfield, Helene Gibbons, Scott Eckers, Marisa Occelli, Jacqueline Lucci, Kim Pritchard, Debi Puccio, Dottie Wolf, Sue Tell-Lindley, Helen Specht-Curley, Kathy Wagner, Kim Wagner, Chuma and Johane Celestin-Ogene, Pascale Kavanagh, Maggie Mouscardy, Jennifer Lowe, Lisa Murray, Melissa D'Angelo, Jacqueline Pradel, Denise Gilles, Brittany Brown, Elizabeth Sheffer Winig, Shelly Larit, Brett Klopp, and Michelle Bushing*

*A special thanks to CreateSpace and the Project Team, especially Whitney.*

This book is dedicated to the future children of America, who are yet to be educated in our public schools.

WE LOVE YOU
MISS McCARTHY!
YOU'RE
THE
BEST!
WE'LL
MISS
YOU!
THANKS
FOR BEING
A GR8
TEACHER

"Miss McCarthy I can't believe that you're retiring!" Chris exclaimed with shock and sadness.

"Oh my goodness, Christopher, how wonderful to see you!! Look how you've grown!! What grade are you in now?"

"I'm a senior - graduating this year! I got accepted into the honors program at the State University!"

"How wonderful! That is quite an accomplishment!! Congratulations, dear!!! And how is your brother, Nick?" inquired Miss McCarthy.

"Nick's good, but Miss McCarthy, what happened? Why is the school being shut down? **I just can't believe it!** This is an awesome school!! **You teachers were great!! Where are the students going to go?** And you, I cannot believe **YOU** of all teachers are retiring!" Chris asked bewildered.

"Sometimes I can't believe it either, sweetheart. Unfortunately, under the state regulations, the school was not showing progress, so we are being **shut down!**"

*"How could you guys let this happen? Where will the kids go?"*

"Chris, we didn't let this happen. The Teachers Union has been fighting this legislation for a very long time. The kids will choose where they want to go. They'll either stay here and go to the new privately corporate-owned charter school, that will be renting the building, or they will choose to go to another public school. Some of the teachers will be reassigned to sub at other public schools, or they'll be hired by a non-union charter school. Personally, I'm just too old to be reassigned to another school as a substitute teacher, and since I am able to retire, it really was my only option," replied Miss McCarthy.

"But I don't understand! This is a good school, and you're the best teacher I've ever had! You were always so willing to help us. Sometimes there were so many kids in your room for extra help that we even had to sit on the floor! Personally, I'll never forget how I was failing English and you always came in early and stayed late just to help me understand what we were learning. Do you know I'm going to be an English major? I want to be a news reporter or a journalist! And it's all because of you!"

"That means so much to me Chris, but what's currently happening in education is not about being the best teacher, or even a good one. And it's certainly not just about me. It's not uncommon for teachers to come in early and to work beyond the school day in order to help our students succeed. Our "bonus" doesn't come in the form of a check; it's an intrinsic reward. Sadly, our profession is losing many talented people who have a lot to contribute to the education system. It's about politics and very wealthy people in this country who are trying to privatize public education so that they can become even richer. They stand to make a lot of money siphoning public funds for private profit."

"I still don't get it!! How are they able to shut down an entire school? And I'm not really sure what you mean by privatize," questioned Chris.

"To privatize, or the act of privatization, means to take something that is owned by the government and to make it privately owned for capitalistic gain. Why don't you sit down, sweetheart, and Miss McCarthy will explain it all to you. It could be your first news story!

It truly is a heartbreak for those of us who believe in public education - especially those of us who have dedicated our lives to making a difference in the lives of children. I've always wanted to be a teacher, you know. There was nothing else I ever wanted to be nor imagined being.

During my childhood, I used to play two things: house and school. My father was opposed to it. He wanted me to go into business with him – 'McCarthy and Daughter' he would have called the business, but that was not meant to be. I **wanted** to be a teacher!

I finally mustered up the courage to stand up to him, and it was one of the best decisions of my life!"

"Do you know that we could always tell, Miss McCarthy, that you loved us and you loved what you did - even when we were misbehaving?" interjected Chris.

"You were children and you acted like children," Miss McCarthy replied with a smile.

"Then why are they closing our school?" asked Chris.

"It really has nothing to do with *us*. In 2001, the George W. Bush administration passed legislation entitled, *NO CHILD LEFT BEHIND*. That required schools to show at a certain point and time, through student testing, that 100 percent of the students were performing at the proficient level in reading, writing and math. Needless to say, it was an impossible feat. Even excellent schools were deemed as failing because of the diverse student population. **Public schools educate everyone, unlike charter schools that can pick and choose their students. Public schools do not discriminate based on a child's IQ or whether or not he or she is an English Language Learner.**"

"That doesn't seem right that some schools can pick and choose who they educate, Miss McCarthy."

"True, and not only that, but charter schools are also exempt from state mandates for the first couple of years while they are establishing themselves. That's why many charters close and then reopen under another name; it buys them more time. *What's even more dangerous about some charter schools is that some are privately owned, yet they are funded with public tax dollars. This takes much needed money away from public schools.*"

"Wow! That means they can actually make money from government funds? Do people realize this? Isn't anyone doing something about it?"

"Yes, it does. And again, the Teachers Union has been working hard to stop it, but the propaganda that's being sold makes it seem as if teachers are against educational reform."

"You know, I never really understood how public schools were funded," replied Chris.

"I'll be happy to explain it to you," Miss McCarthy smiled as she continued.

"Public schools are funded with federal and state tax dollars. That's what partly got us into this mess. When the Obama Administration came in, they implemented *RACE TO THE TOP*, which promised states billions of dollars if they implemented the **Common Core Standards** – privately developed standards that are *voluntarily* adopted by a state in order to get the funding.

A main goal of the Standards is College and Career Readiness. However, in adopting the Standards, states also adopt **Key Instructional Shifts.** For example, one shift proposes a balance of literary fiction and non-fiction from kindergarten to fifth grade but much more focus on the non-fiction in grades six through twelve in order to prepare students for college and future careers - as if literature can't be used to prepare you for the future!"

"I remember when we used to read stories and poems in class; you would always say that art mirrors life and understanding the author's message would help us to understand ourselves and the world we live in. I've never forgotten that. It's helped me a lot because I try to be like Atticus Finch - especially at work with disgruntled customers."

"That's a perfect example of what I'm talking about, Chris. See how helpful that is to you? Literature can not only be used to learn to think critically, but it can also be used to learn about humanity. Even though the proposed shift is to teach more and more non-fiction as you kids get into the upper grades, in all fairness, **To Kill a Mockingbird** is actually a state module. That being said, however, it has been a staple in many English classrooms for decades."

"Really? So to get federal funding, states have to go along with this?"

"Yes, they do."

"Now, what about state funding?"

"As for state tax dollars, each state funds its schools differently. In our state, every year schools put forth a budget and their communities vote on it. Recently, in New York, the governor proposed a state tax cap of two percent, which the state legislature passed, and he then signed into law. The cap means schools cannot increase their budget by more than two percent unless it's passed by a super majority. People don't realize that, even with the tax cap, schools have to implement the state mandates which are tied to **RACE TO THE TOP**. This costs a lot of money, not to mention other increases in expenditures that can happen every year, such as health care, necessary repairs to buildings, and the like. **Due to the tax cap, schools have had to cut educational programs and even increase class sizes in order to stay within their budgets.**

The other difficult thing is that passing a budget is emotionally charged. The public doesn't have much sympathy for teachers because conditions in the private sector are very different, and it can feel very unfair. Many people in the private sector have not gotten raises for many years, and they've lost some of their benefits, like their pensions. So they feel that teachers have it too good. The truth is that they should never have been allowed to lose their pensions."

"I remember reading about the Enron scandal in history class. It was terrible how that corporation lied to stockholders and then lost the money they had invested," replied Chris.

"Yes, that was definitely an adverse turning point for workers, and it also showed us how far corporations will go to make a profit. The other issue is that voting 'NO' on a school budget allows people who are angry about what is happening, with the economy and the government, to voice their unhappiness – sadly, at the risk of hurting their schools."

"I wonder how many times Congress would actually get a pay raise if the American people could vote on their budget," laughed Chris.

"Not many! If we truly want to help the public school system in America, one of the first things we need to do is to revamp the whole idea of voting on school budgets. We also have to let our elected officials know that we want them to **support our public schools**," added Miss McCarthy.

"I say we vote on Congress' budget instead!" Chris continued.

"Me too," giggled Miss McCarthy.

"Now you mentioned ***RACE TO THE TOP***; what's that?" asked Chris.

"Do you remember what I told you about ***NO CHILD LEFT BEHIND*** and people wanting to make a lot of money by privatizing education? ***RACE TO THE TOP is NO CHILD LEFT BEHIND*** run amuck!

***NO CHILD LEFT BEHIND*** gave privately owned corporations the opportunity to make a lot of money through test development and charter schools. This blossomed because public schools were being deemed as ineffective since they couldn't meet the impossible goals established for them. However,

when the Obama Administration took office, they dangled **a five billion dollar** carrot in front of states if they implemented *RACE TO THE TOP*.

In order to get this money, states had to agree to: **1. Implement the Common Core Standards, 2. Evaluate teachers by using their students' test scores, 3. Increase the number of charter schools in their state**, and **4. Improve their lowest performing schools - even if it meant closing PUBLIC schools!**

Chris, the questions you have to ask yourself for your news article are:
*Where did these standards come from?*
*Who was behind their development?*
*Who would be developing the tests, and why would they be linked to a teacher's evaluation?*
*Who would be opening these charter schools, and who would be improving these 'failing' schools?*

What made matters worse is that, according to *RACE TO THE TOP*, schools are rated by student achievement on these standardized tests and could be labeled failing if *students* don't show growth through testing."

"It isn't reasonable or even logical to expect anything to show consistent growth like that! **Why would high performing schools even be threatened in that way?** Are corporations and businesses tested and then shut down when they don't show consistent growth?" exclaimed Chris.

"You're 100% right! That's because it really has nothing to do with truly improving education. It's all about money, and lots of it!" Miss McCarthy continued.

"Corporate America has often dictated national policy. These 'Corporate Reformers' have used propaganda to sell the American people on the idea that public education is broken, and **nothing could be further from the truth**. True, there are things that need improvement, but public education in America has never been better. More kids are graduating than ever before, and we are educating a broader spectrum of people than ever before. What's actually worse is that you have some really good districts, like ours, that are being destroyed. There's a lot of money to be made developing tests, scoring tests, publishing workbooks and promoting fear - **all with the taxpayer footing the bill!**

You also have to remember, people move into areas because of the schools. So when the scores come out in the paper, if they are not considered to be good scores, potential buyers shy away from those

districts. **What many people fail to realize is that the scores can vary dramatically based on demographics.**

For example, a district with a lot of English Language Learners may be an excellent district, and yet not score as well as another. An English Language Learner could be deemed proficient enough in English to take the test, but may not be as versed in our culture as someone who was born here. This puts the child at a disadvantage when taking the test - even if he/she is attending a wonderful school where he/she is excelling academically."

"WOW," responded Chris, "I never realized that before! We should be doing something about this!!"

"Yes, you should - we all should. And you should start by contacting your elected officials and telling them to **support public education**. I also hope to see that news article printed, Mr. English Major!"

"Now Chris, I've told you, the Teachers Union has been fighting this for quite some time, but unfortunately, the public thinks it's just because of how it's affecting us. It wasn't until the testing became so emotionally brutal for students that there was a public outcry, and people pushed back."

"Geez, I remember **ALL** those tests!! It was ridiculous and terrible! For years, **we had to take tests in so many subjects**! I remember thinking how stressful it was to have to take a test in art, music, and phys ed! It took away so much instructional time. The worst ones were the math and English tests. They were impossible, and I remember how stressed out everyone got. Spring had always been my favorite time in school until it became **nothing but testing**!  Do you remember the day that Sofi cried?"

"You bet I do! I felt terrible. Poor little thing, she was so overwhelmed. She had such test anxiety and thought she was not smart because she didn't have time to finish the test on the first day. She was only one of many. I cannot begin to tell you how many children become demoralized because of those tests. **Here we are trying to take care of the 'whole' child, helping kids to grow into confident, self-assured young adults and these tests tear them down. It's ludicrous to think of children who barely know how to read or write, being forced to learn how to bubble in a Scantron**! No matter what they say, these tests encourage teachers to 'teach to the test' and promote stress!"

"Yeah, I know. My cousin, Phillip, is having a really hard time in school right now. I overheard my mom and aunt talking. Apparently, Phillip told my aunt that he was stupid because he couldn't do well on any of these tests. He refused to go to school. My aunt had to take him to a doctor for his growing anxiety. Phillip actually told my aunt that maybe he'd be better off in heaven. He's on medication now. My aunt told my mom that she wasn't going to let my cousin take the test any more - especially since she doesn't think it really has anything to do with him and his education. They were both crying."

"That is terrible, but unfortunately, it's not the first time I've heard this. That is her right; however, I'd rather see your aunt write to her state representatives to work toward making the test what it was intended to be – a true educational diagnostic instrument to help, not hurt, children. What grade is Phillip in now?" asked Miss McCarthy.

"He's in fourth," continued Chris.

"What a shame!"

"So, Miss McCarthy, what happens to kids who don't pass the test or can't?"

"Good question. Currently, they are being remediated, that is, given additional help. The statistics on Academic Intervention Services are staggering, but even with AIS, some kids just can't do it.

You know, there's one thing that I've never understood as an educator. We embrace every kind of diversity in this country except for intellectual diversity; everyone has to be brilliant. Well, that's just not the way the world is. Not only that, but there are multiple intelligences. How can you be a genius on all fronts?"

"Maybe if we all recognized that, everyone would be happier, and there would be a lot less stress!" interjected Chris.

"Don't get me wrong; I most certainly believe in the importance of a fundamental education, but I also know many successful, happy people who didn't go down the common path."

"Yeah, Steve Jobs was one of them!" Chris added.

"Unbelievably, even as parents and concerned individuals are becoming aware of what is happening to our educational system and are voicing their opposition, the testing movement still seems to be moving full-steam ahead! **PARCC** (The Partnership for Assessment of Readiness College and Careers) has already field tested over a million children, and according to them, are ready to administer assessments to all children, under the pretext of 'fixing' public education."

"That's a lot of tests Miss McCarthy!"

"Yep! A lot of public money to be made by the private sector! You know, Chris, people are happy and successful in all lines of work. Our society would not be able to function if we all did the same thing. So it's ludicrous to expect children to be perfect students and then hold their teachers accountable for it when they are not. It's also ridiculous to require a seventh grader to score well on a test that adults have difficulty passing."

"Some of those test questions were really confusing and the passages were so long. I remember a lot of my friends didn't think they did as well as they thought they could have because they didn't even have time to finish the test. Ugh!! Those really were the **WORST** days in school!! I wish my mom could have seen what my assessments were like; maybe she wouldn't have been so upset with me when I didn't do as well as she thought I should have."

"Well, she can now. All she would have to do is to go on the **PARCC** website, and she would be able to actually take a sample assessment. There is also the **SBAC** (SMARTER Balanced Assessment Consortium) which students may be able to take, but the public, in our state, doesn't know too much about that even being a viable option."

"Miss McCarthy, you said that teachers were evaluated based on student test scores? I never realized that - is that true?"

"Very much so, Chris. If the students don't show growth on their test scores – even if you are an excellent teacher, eventually a teacher could be fired! I think the reason you probably didn't realize it is because many of us don't want to add to the pressure you kids feel. **It's also an extremely unprofessional way to evaluate teachers!**"

"*That's OUTRAGEOUS*! It's kind of like evaluating a doctor by how many of his patients actually get better. What if the patient doesn't do what the doctor recommended, or what if the doctor treated terminally ill patients? Would that mean that doctor was ineffective? **That's definitely going to be in my news article!" exclaimed Chris.**

"Sounds good to me! Not all students are good test takers. I have had some A, A+ students actually score below the proficient line; then there are the ones who are so sick of taking tests that they just don't try. It also doesn't seem to matter that every year the pool of students changes. Some years I had many more students with special needs than other years. Did that mean that I was a better or a worse teacher those years?"

"You could never be a bad teacher Miss McCarthy!! I really did love all the stories and books we read and how you used them to teach us lessons about life, and how to be better human beings, and how to make good choices. Why aren't we investing in people?"

"**Teaching is more than disseminating information and being scripted**. It's developing lessons that allow students to expand their minds so that they can take knowledge and go beyond. And it's definitely more than just testing and data collection. I think it's also about connecting with your kids, **showing them how that knowledge applies to their lives, and how to transfer the skills they gain to new situations.**

The **ultimate goal** of education shouldn't be to prepare the individual for personal success. **It is to make him/her a positive and successful contributor to society**. For example, informational text will teach you how to succeed at building the shelf you bought from IKEA. But like you said Chris, the book, *To Kill a Mockingbird*, will teach you the importance of understanding people who are seemingly different from you so that you can find a common ground, respect one another and socially coexist.

Teachers lose so much instructional time preparing students for these tests. Whether it's in the form of the curriculum we are being given or test prep, **we are losing the humanity in education!**"

"It's definitely what you taught us! You helped me to see, even as a seventh grader, that what I was learning was important and would have relevance in my future and in life. And it did!" said a voice at the door.

"Nick!!" exclaimed Miss McCarthy.

"Hey, what are you doing here, bro?" asked Chris, as his brother embraced Miss McCarthy.

"Mom said you had come to say goodbye to Miss McCarthy because she was retiring so I wanted to also," replied Nick.

"How are your parents?"

"They're fine, annoying! Always pushing me to do more!"

"Then they're doing their job," laughed Miss McCarthy.

"I still can't believe you taught my mom," Chris interjected.

"Yep! I have had the honor of teaching your mom, your brother, and you. It goes fast!"

"I was hoping you'd teach my kids," said Nick, "but now that the school's closing, I guess none of my old teachers will! It's so crazy!! I **NEVER** imagined that this school would ever close!!

"That's what we were just talking about, Nick. Miss McCarthy was just telling me about how people are trying to privatize education by making public schools look bad because they can personally make a lot of money!" replied Chris.

"But don't you have tenure, Miss McCarthy? **I thought if you had tenure, you could never lose your job.**"

Miss McCarthy laughed, "I see I've got my work cut out for me today!! Yes, I do have tenure, but that does not mean I can't get fired or that I have a job for life! **The only thing that tenure grants is due process. ALL government employees have the right to due process.**"

"What do you mean by 'due process'?" asked Chris.

"That means that my boss can't just come in one morning and fire me because he or she feels like it, which is the way it can be in the private sector. If my boss thinks I'm not doing my job, then she has to prove that I'm not doing it at a hearing. If I'm found to be guilty of not doing my job after the hearing, then I can be let go. Unfortunately, the way the law was written made it difficult for supervisors to prove that teachers, who were not doing their jobs, were incompetent. Since then, the law has been changed to make it more equitable for everyone. Trust me, **hard-working teachers don't appreciate it when our reputation as educators gets tarnished.**"

"So then what is the point of tenure?" asked Nick.

**Tenure protects schools and teachers from indiscriminately being let go which causes a lot of turnover and can have a negative impact on schooling. This also permits teachers to have academic freedom so that we can teach appropriate material without fear of censorship. It allows teachers to stand up for what we believe in, and it also allows us to protect our students if we need to.**"

"Didn't we read something about evolution and some guy who got arrested for teaching it?"

"Excellent memory, Nick! Yes, we did. We read about John T. Scopes - that's a perfect example of why tenure is so important."

"If that's the case, then why are people trying to take away tenure from teachers?"

"Wow! You boys are definitely as smart as I remember! **Trying to take away teachers' tenure is really a veiled attempt at union busting**. It's a back door way of getting rid of teachers. Our union fights to protect public education, and if you weaken the union, it would be a lot easier to privatize education. You see, **if you can show that teachers are ineffective by having them evaluated by using variable student test performance and having to show growth - an extremely inequitable, if not unrealistic requirement - then you can fire them whether or not they have tenure**."

"How sneaky - that's definitely going into my news article about saving public education!" exclaimed Chris.

"But who writes these tests?"

"The process is overseen by the state's education department. Most of the education department employees I've ever worked with were very caring and dedicated individuals. However, the actual development of the math and English Assessments is contracted out."

"So, you mean the tests aren't even written by teachers?"

"I'm sure some of the company's employees have had some educational training, but in general, no. What they do is consult with teachers at various points of test development."

"Wow - if you think about every student in the state, or better yet in the country, having to take these tests, that's a lot of tests!!"

"And a lot of money to be made," added Chris.

"Corporations are not just developing these tests. They're also behind the development of the **Common Core Standards** which states were enticed to adopt, and over the years, they've developed curriculum too. Go on this website - www.engageny.org. You'll be able to see how far reaching the arm of corporate America stretches into education."

"I **REALLY** don't get why people are allowing this to happen!! Don't they think **public education is important**?" asked Chris.

"I think that most people are unaware, and sadly, there isn't much sympathy for teachers, Chris. However, it's not just about the teachers. Until just recently there was a company called inBloom that processed student demographic and personal information for social marketing. Thankfully, when parents found out about it, there was a huge movement to prevent your information from being used for profit so that company went out of business."

"I'll have to ask my mom if she heard about that. Well, I have to tell you, all the teachers I've had were very hard working; that's why I still can't believe they're closing this school! That's also why we have to do something to keep this from happening to other schools! I'm starting with writing to my state senator about what I've learned today!" said Nick.

"That's great, and I definitely agree with you! As a whole, **teachers are very hard working and caring individuals**. So much so, in fact, that many of them don't get involved in the whole political uproar; they're too busy working hard at teaching. Since the situation has gotten so dire, I'm sure they'll be more active! **Everyone's busy, but we all have time to make a phone call, write a letter, or send an email or a fax!**

**What truly worries me is the future of public education in America. Granted, the school system is not perfect, but like I said, it's not as broken as those behind the privatization movement would have you believe.** I'm afraid kids won't want to be teachers in the future. As it is, there are so many requirements that for all the time, energy and money they would have to invest in becoming a teacher, they could become doctors or lawyers, and those professions would be far more lucrative."

"That's a shame because we can always use highly educated and dedicated people in education," said Nick.

"Yes, we most certainly can, sweetheart. People are forgetting that throughout history, schools have played a vital role in our society. As a matter of fact, it has been a little bit of a double-edged sword for us. **People look to schools as a venue to fix many social issues. Unfortunately, educators are not given the freedom nor the resources to do so, and IT'S THE CHILDREN WHO SUFFER.**

**Our children have been crying out in so many ways; I don't know why we're not hearing them.** Ultimately, the goal of education is to produce positive successful contributors to society through personal growth, intellectual stimulation and enlightenment.

"Is there anything else we can do?" asked Nick.

"Of course! You can take action! Here's what you can do:

1. *Stay current and informed about the issues.*
2. *Write to your state representatives and let them know how you want to be represented.*
3. *Get in touch with your local schools and Parent-Teacher Associations to find out what you can do to support public education in your community."*

"We can definitely do that, right boys?"

"Mom!!"

"Kate, how nice to see you," said Miss McCarthy.

"Well, I couldn't let the boys come say goodbye and not do so myself. I hope they did not overstay their welcome, Miss McCarthy."

"Not at all, and please, I think you could call me by my first name, Marina," Miss McCarthy replied.

"Mom, Miss McCarthy was telling us the real reason they were closing the school, and it's terrible," said Nick.

"Somehow I can't imagine you being retired, Marina."

"You're definitely right there. Although I won't be teaching anymore, I will still be pretty busy. I'm going to be working with my local school district and the Teachers Union to raise public awareness regarding what's currently happening in public education, and more importantly, how all this testing and so-called educational reform is adversely affecting our children with this unwarranted stress."

"Well, I'm going to do my part to save public education - starting with this news article for the local paper!" interjected Chris.

"You can tell me all about what you've learned on the way home."

"We definitely will," said Nick, "and when I get home, **I'm emailing my state senator**!"

"Boys, I'm sure you'll tell me what I can do to help!"

"You bet Mom!!" the boys said in unison.

"Thanks, Marina. Even retired, you're still educating us!"

"Thank you for coming to say goodbye and for helping teachers to ***SPREAD THE WORD!***"

Together we can get to the core of the issue

and

SUPPORT PUBLIC EDUCATION!!!

# Save Our Public Schools Action Plan
## Miss McCarthy Suggests:

- ☐ I will advocate for our children's right to a public education and help others to do the same!

- ☐ I will know who state and national representatives are and how to contact them!

- ☐ I will write to my representatives and let them know how to represent me!

- ☐ I will join the district Parent-Teacher Association and attend meetings - be active and aware!

- ☐ I will attend School Board Meetings - in order to be active and aware!

- ☐ I will find out if there is a district Parent-Teacher Liaison Committee working together to meet students' needs. If yes, I will get involved! If not, I will start one!

- ☐ I will find out how assessments and mandates actually impact the educational process in my home school district.

- ☐ I will take practice PARCC and Smarter Balanced assessments to understand what is expected of children and when.

# Save Our Public Schools Action Plan
## My Achievement Goals:

- ☐ _____
- ☐ _____
- ☐ _____
- ☐ _____
- ☐ _____
- ☐ _____
- ☐ _____
- ☐ _____
- ☐ _____
- ☐ _____

A lot of money is going into "fixing" public education.

How much of it is actually being used to help our children?

Here are some websites you may wish to visit in your quest for higher knowledge:

http://www.parcconline.org/

http://www.smarterbalanced.org/

http://www.ccsso.org/

http://www.corestandards.org/http://www.ccsso.org/

http://www.achieve.org/achieving-common-core

http://elschools.org/

http://www.washingtonpost.com/blogs/answer-sheet/wp/2013/05/12/gates-give-150-million-in-grants-for-common-core-standards/

http://www.gatesfoundation.org/What-We-Do/US-Program/College-Ready-Education

http://www.nga.org/cms/home/news-room/news-releases/page_2009/col2-content/main-content-list/title_common-core-state-standards-initiative-validation-committee-announced.html

http://www.alternet.org/education/who-profiting-charters-big-bucks-behind-charter-school-secrecy-financial-scandal-and

http://www.uncommonschools.org/faq-what-is-charter-school

http://dianeravitch.net/

http://www.missmccarthy.com

If you liked Miss McCarthy's message, help her spread the word!!

Books available for purchase at www.CreateSpace.com/ 5247867, Amazon.com and www.missmccarthy.com.

## Ode to John Dewey

Young and nervous -
Tightly holding on to pen and notebook,
I entered the hallowed halls of academia.

Bodies filed in -
One by one each seat was occupied.

Looking around, yet looking away -
We acknowledged each other's presence.

I sat silently waiting for the holder of all wisdom…
to speak,
to instill within me everything the universe expected me to learn.

Wasn't that why I was here -
to be inducted into the hallowed halls of the intelligentsia?

> *"Education is not preparation for life; education is life itself."*[1]

A hush wavered above,
The room felt eerily still…

*"Give the pupils something to do, not something to learn; and the doing is of such a nature as to demand thinking; learning naturally results."*[2]

Each quote drew me in -
nearer to the reasons, the understanding, the truth.

I had been warned -
told to be careful, yet I was finding my calling - fast and furious!!

*"I do not see how any honest educational reformer in western countries can deny that the greatest practical obstacle in the way of introducing into schools that connection with social life which he regards as desirable is the great part played by personal competition and desire for private profit in our economic life. This fact almost makes it necessary that in important respects school activities should be protected from social contacts and connections, instead of being organized to create them."*[3]

"So, what do you think?" my professor inquired.
She…she wants ME to think?
MY…MY thoughts matter!

Tania Mouscardy-Johnson, 2014

1 - 3  http://www.goodreads.com/author/quotes/42738.John_Dewey

About the Author: **Tania Mouscardy-Johnson**
*P.D. Educational Administration*
*M.A. Secondary English Education*
*B.S. Secondary English Education/ Business Communications Minor*

As a thirty year career educator who has enjoyed an outstanding and successful tenure at one of New York State's highly acclaimed school districts, Tania Mouscardy-Johnson is committed to children and excellence in education. She has served as an educational consultant for New York State Education Department on numerous committees and was a member of the New York State Regents' Standards Review Initiative, as well as the New York State Regents' Common Core Review Initiative. For the past twenty-five years, Ms. Mouscardy-Johnson has served and continues to serve as a NYSUT local representative, as well as on countless district-based committees. She is also the proud recipient of the PTSA Jenkins' Award for her dedication to her students and her profession. Although there are challenges to overcome, Ms. Mouscardy- Johnson whole-heartedly believes in the ability of American public education to meet the intellectual, emotional, social, and creative needs of America's children.

About the Illustrator: **Luanne Rozran**

Although Luanne Rozran is not new to the world of illustration, above all she considers herself an artist in every sense of the word. She is an impressionist who uses her art to tell a story. In this particular work, it is used to help clarify what has needed to be said about American public education for quite some time. Mrs. Rozran's personal story can be found in "Violet Finds her Place in the Rainbow". Her work may also be seen in "Orange Finds his Place in the Rainbow" written by her husband, Jeffrey Rozran. Other works may be found at www.newyorkflair.vpweb.com.

www.ingramcontent.com/pod-product-compliance
Lightning Source LLC
Chambersburg PA
CBHW041226040426
42444CB00002B/62